MINSTRELSY

THE SONGS OF THE SOUL

FORAM PATEL

Made with ♥ on the Notion Press Platform
www.notionpress.com

Dedicated to

My Brother, Amit.

The Man

who could adore

women a lot.

Love and Blessings

wherever he is.

Contents

Contents

Preface

'Minstrelsy' is a production of sentiments with a pal of mind. Poetry to me is a natural flow, a mood, and then a sitting on process of drafting, revising, polishing and so on. When you're writing successfully, being "in the zone" is enjoyable and effortless, and God Knows anything can and frequently does come up from anywhere. These poems are the triggers coming from a heart and mind of woman who has been through a lot: a lot of observations, psychedelic, serene and mystical experiences. The never-ending saga of emotions: it soothes sparkles, speaks and blasts too at times.

I'm not a writer, mostly: I'm living my simple life, managing and getting on with the things as and when I happen to receive them. Abrupt realignments and writing inclinations are inherently enigmatic and tend to be rude and fragmented. I don't frequently try to will myself into a state that will allow me to write. The triggers—those tiny clicks that make you want to stop what you're doing and start writing—have always struck me as being utterly random.

'Chime' might be a better verb. A concept or emotion that you hadn't previously experienced in a given situation or relationship snaps into place and everything feels harmonic and somewhat realigned. I'm not making any major originality claims; as long as it resonates with me as a revelation, it's important. I also don't follow any predetermined routines or "poem traps." For me, skipping, squirming out of things that needed doing, and carving out time in an already hectic day has been a big part of creating poetry.

I believe, the more you observe, the deeper you understand and the better you write. My enjambment might have fragments of words, but are tried upon the finished emotional going-through. The rhythmos, typography, sound, imagery, and ideas–while you write a poem are your surroundings. Although "Minstrelsy" is a fee-flow: a flow of mood and emotions, observations and sequels.

Did I know what a monostich (one line), a couplet (two lines), a tercet or triplet (three lines), and or quatrain (four lines) mean in writing of the poem? Not really. But when you learn them and still prefer to write your poems in free-verse, it is fluid and reader-friendly. When writing of it comes so easily that afterwards I wonder why I don't write poems all the time. When I was very young, I found it very difficult to go through a line of the poem and catch the intentions of the writer. So thought I, my first poetry should be written and composed in a way anybody can read and comprehend. If you resonate and feel through my words, the writing of these poems is successful.

Foram Patel

'Minstrelsy' (A Collection of 35-Poems)

Acknowledgements

I thank the spirit in me, my God in and out, a constant force and a continual source of inspiration. My indebt gratitude to my Guru, parents and my loving late brother who have stood by me no matter what.

My sincere thanks to my friends, who are the soul part of my life and not less than my family. They are the ones I have opened myself truly and have exchanged ourselves.

I owe them and my life journey a lot to thank for.

Thanks much. Love.

Prologue

"Minstrelsy" is a collection of 35-poems written originally in English. The poems in the collection are written in the different times of the writer's life.

The collection does not claim to be original as the idea, this or the other way, is a form of inspiration from the world, people, writing, media the eyes and mind get travel to.

The emotions are tried upon the verbetim keeping in mind the limitations of the writer's knowledge of the words, their meanings, usage and content.

Looking forward to receiving good amount of response from the readers.

1. Value It.

She once said,
'I do that for me', 'for my good and well-being.'
And I understood now
what it is- Value your 'beinghood'
Value your emotions; for they are power in you,
Value your words; for they are what you make out of you,
Value the time: for it's a commodity,
Value the essence; for it is the only thing that lasts,
Value the surroundings; for it is what makes life,
Value the people; for they make society,
Value the mates; for they make the difference,
Value your actions, for they bring results,
Value the inhabitors, for they make living,
Value the objects; for they make use of your limbs,
Value the breath; for what you live for,
Value yourself; for what your struggles are intended to end up.
Value the presence; for it is what it is. Live it.

2. Labels

Life is like
a heady wine, a colored one
Everyone reads the label
on the bottle
Hardly anyone tastes
the wine.
The taste of water
Take as liquor, a cry, a drop, a life!
If we would only 'taste'
a song of the bird,
a smell of the flower,
a shadow of the tree,
a rain-drop,
a bit beat,
a tear ? or
a human eye!
But alas, we have no time . . .
We are spent
deciphering the labels.

3. The Reunion

The topper of the class
Is a Happy Homemaker.
The backbencher of the lot
Is an Entrepreneur.
The Flamboyant fashionista,
Became a dreaded Lawyer.
Often ignored Anita
Turned into a well-known Writer.
The overlooked Shiba
Is an excellent content writer.
The one who failed English Paper two times,
Became an English Professor.
The one who failed in the maths paper
Is a Chartered Accountant.
The one - a simple and shabby Shrina
Is a Fashion Designer in now!
And the one who often got to stand outside,
Is an Army officer.
The reunion taught all of us:
People come with many layers,
Not to judge
A books by the cover,
The scores, a grade card,

The clothes, lifestyle,
A style, the character,
The ways, the personality,
The past, the person
The present, the future.
You never know, what is next.
Each child out there has a
Unique success story…!!!

4. Can We Stop?

Can we stop with how much we bear?
And, how much we react to it!
Can we stop waiting the long days and,
Reckless nights,
Can we stop shouting at loved ones?
Can we stop being the so-called good person,
And bearing the silence against their misdeeds,
Can we stop others from taking advantage of our kindness?
Can we stop regretting our past!
Can we stop holding onto grieves that have broken us into pieces?
Can we stop trusting the flow of time
And start believing that you will have to value the moments?
Can we stop chasing after people and being the only fixers
And let them take the equal weight?
Can we stop ourselves to reach the peaks of our suffering?
And start breaking the belief - 'one-day things may improve'?
Can we stop going with the flow and making our own paths,
And take back the power in our hands to lead our lives the way we want?
Can we stop people titling us and our gesture this or that?
And start making them sees clearly what we actually are?
Can we stop creating our own storms?

And feel the journey for what may come?
Are we willing to suffer in silence for other people?
Can we learn and start saying 'no'?
Can we get more comfortable with our disagreements on things?
And start enjoying the world inside us and indeed outside us?
Can we break the stereotypes of leading a life with someone?
And start making ourselves a good pal for ourselves?
Can we stop behaving with people - "'I am 'okay'" and "'fine'"?
Can we straight talk and say- I am going through this?
Can we clear our boundaries and keep the passage clean?
Can we simply simplify life and live free?
Can we do these all? Yes, we shall do these all.
Ourselves.
On our own.
Let's do that.

5. Their Coffee!

Whose Coffee is that?!
Your or mine! I think I know!
It was a debt to rain!
The first coffee and us!
The owner is quite happy though.
With the regular visitors,
Full of joy, the souls of rain.
Happy are they,
One at the coffee time & the other at the sight.
They laugh, cry hello, and the day- bliss!
She gives her coffee a shake,
And laughs until her belly aches,
The only other sound is the break,
'How was your day?'
'Crazy busy' as usual!
The coffee eases them
It is fun, wise, and deep,
But they have promises to keep,
Mails, dogs, kids, parents, bla bla la la li la…
They sing the song of home and work.
Rest and sleep are costlier with them,
Yet they cheer each other up, on the coffee table,
It is break time

Cheers to the talks and friendship they share
End the day with a coffee.
Ready for the next day.

6. Teach the Little One

Teach a little one,
To be a man and a woman:
Teach a little why and how
To respect the underhood
To turn into beinghood.
Teach a little one
The difference between a girl and a woman
The difference between a boy and a man,
Teach a little one how to see the world,
Show them the world of generosity and humanity.
Teach a little one
To hold the hand of a man in trouble,
To stand by one's shabby and scuffled phase,
To touch the heart of people.
Teach a little one
To ride the waves to land,
To draw the lines
To say no whenever time pleases,
To adjust and survive.
Teach a little one, so that the mind will learn,
To adapt to - 'it is fine, I don't need to fight for everything!'
To accept - 'all of us struggle!"
To believe and act upon - 'Healing is my responsibility."

To stop - "blame games".
Teach a little one,
To take little steps,
To walk with open eyes,
To offer a helping hand.
Teach a little one,
words are his own,
They will impact his life.
Teach a little one to feel,
His heart not to conceal,
Help him to be okay with his eyes,
Filled with tears,
and a heart with pain,
that they can be their strength and not weakness.
Teach a little one,
The lesson of forgiving and healing,
The fun with nature,
The serenity and beauty,
And love of travel.
Teach a little one,
The meanings of words,
Culture, peace, and life.
Teach a little one,
To go with the flow.
Teach a little one,
This life is a journey of beinghood,
And not a race of destination.

7. Intimacy

Intimacy
Is not who you talk to
Is not who you lie to
Is not who you hide things from,
Is not you think twice before texting
Or calling;
Is not the feeling of friction in the body,
Fear in the eyes,
Is not quarreling for the rights and needs instead
Is not spending heedless days-and-nights
Is not talking about it to the third,
Is not about your yearning for the person,
Is not about the fact of being together for
Years, months, days
Is not about the number of pictures you have,
Is not about eating and sleeping together,
Neither about the titles you share.
Is about the care and concern you have,
Is about your fearlessness to approach them untimely,
Is about sharing how that tea tested, and the man at the door,
Sharing and swapping the stories of the day,
About how tiring the work is
And how a new job feels like,

Is about sharing the bucket list,
Is about planning the rand
Is about faith in one another,
Is about the value you share for the other
Is about adoring one's existence
And absence as well,
Is about the attention you give,
Is about the appreciation you make,
Is about valuing one another,
Is about the care and concern you can't take away,
From the head and heart.
Is about the feeling that
May fluctuate,
But shall never die.
Intimacy is that oneness you share in every talk,
Intimacy is the openness between the minds and souls.

8. Fine!

Life is unfair!
When was it fair?!
Fine. It is.
You love them,
They have people they love,
Fine. Keep it fine.
You wait, they don't come back,
Did they tell you to wait?
Fine. It should be fine.
You struggle and survive,
That's how we grow,
Fine. Continue.
You thrust and thrive,
That's how you learn,
Fine. Required.
You break and cry,
That's how we learn whom not to trust,
Fine, You will have to repeat that.
People come and go,
Can you handle them altogether?
Fine. Let them clear the channel.
Stay tuned.
Enjoy the rhythm of

Up and down, dark and light
Blue and white, merry and fairy
Fall and grow:
That's the music. Keep singing.

9. Nurture

Nurture your observations for
What you see,
What you look at,
What you look for,
Where you are,
And not for why you are,
And how it works.
Nurture the journey and not the destination,
Nurture the vision and not the trials,
Nurture the sight and not the show,
Nurture the process and not the runs,
Things take time, believe!
Nurture the belongings and essence,
Nurture your beinghood,
Nurture your origin,
Nurture your instincts,
Nurture the love inside you.
Nurture those souls,
Who love you for what you are, for they love your existence,
For they accept how you react and behave,
For they don't stop you,
For not that they need and want you,
Or for that you complete them.

Nurture the love and care you get
Nurture the concerns. Nurture the love in them.

10. Forgot, Don't!

Don't forget the bad chapters,
For they have made you what you are today.
Don't forget the failures of the plans,
For they have taught you what not to do the next time.
Don't forget about how you have changed,
For this change was required.
Don't forget how far you've come.
Don't forget what you have been through,
Don't forget your push and the struggles
Even when you felt you couldn't.
Don't forget it was you,
Who got out of the bed
Even when you were not well,
Don't forget you handled them,
When things nearly collapsed.
Don't forget you've been your strength,
You, your spirit, the woman in you,
The strong soul and a controlled mind: that cocktail of you,
Don't forget, you needed to be there.
Despite what was out of control,
Don't forget you did well, you gave your best.
At least, you tried. you did.
Don't forget your 'never-giving-up' spirit,

Don't forget you have inspired many, and are yet to go.
Don't forget how they have left,
Don't forget when they have left,
Broke and tore you,
The tears and the scars,
They are part of your learning.
Don't forget you live with yourself,
And not anyone else,
Be your own companion,
Be content with yourself,
Be at peace with yourself.
Don't forget to live for yourself,
Don't forget the learnings,
Don't repeat them, for you learned enough of it,
Don't forget to remind yourself: it was needed, it has to be.
Don't forget you have always tried and succeeded.
Don't forget to retain faith in yourself:
Don't forget to cheer yourself,
Do that for you: again and again.
Don't forget anything.
The scars and scratches; may stay
On the head and in the heart;
let it be: it is part of you.
Let it stay with you. Make some space for it. You will be okay, sis!
But don't forget to forgive them,
For your peace, serenity, and a good life.

Heal and Move on.

11. You Are Enough!

You woke up this morning
Feeling like you didn't get enough sleep,
But you got up.
That's enough.
You went through your day
Believing you didn't put in enough of your energy,
But you gave every ounce you had to give.
That's enough.
You worried that how shall that happen,
Seeing the risks and did think of the other side,
But you tried and appealed.
That's enough.
You worried that your family didn't eat enough healthy means,
But they were fed.
That's enough.
You lay your head down at night,
Replaying all the things you didn't do well enough,
But you did the best you could.
That's enough.
You will never please all at once.
You will never do it all together.
You will not make them work every time.

You can't make it work every time.
You can't do it perfectly right all the way,
But you always tried, you showed up. And that's Enough.

12. Someday

Someday,
Everything will make perfect sense,
So for now,
Laugh at the confusion,
Smile through the tears,
Be strong and keep going,
Enjoy the rain,
Enjoy the meals,
Watch the drama,
Keep reminding yourself,
You are on Earth,
For yourself
To live and cherish.
Someday, you will smile
You did it right.
Someday, you need a break.
Pause, take a break.
Stop, be still a moment.
Let the smell of early morning
Soak you into your lungs
And enliven you.
Let the fresh air of the evening today
Wash over you

Like ocean water under the feet.
Let yourself be calm,
Serene, at peace,
Some day you need music;
Some day you need lyrics,
All the days are not the same.
Let the moments of the day
Wash over you,
And the water will dry
And you will live again.
Make it today.
Make someday a good day.

13. Fear

A river trembles before meeting the sea,
A body shivers before getting onto the stage,
A mind baffles before proposing an idea,
A heart breaks before making a love
The paths are always challenging,
This or the other way,
You will have to travel,
And choose it.
To go back is impossible,
See in the ocean so vast and wide,
Sit there side inside,
We take risks, we need to.
You can't go back,
And that's fine.
There is no other way,
The river or you can't go back.
Enter the ocean,
Feel, drown, swim and you will see
Your fear is disappearing.
That's how you will know
That you have not disappeared:
You have become the ocean now.

14. No Right Time!

Felt that always: 'I was late';
When I got enough confidence,
The stage was gone;
When I was convinced of losing,
I won;
When I needed them the most,
They've gone;
When I learned to dry my tears,
Had the shoulder to lean and cry on;
When I mastered the skill of accepting things, people, and situations the way they are,
Had people who were ready to change their world for me;
When I gave up waiting for the light,
The sun rose and I was asleep,
That is LIFE. Vice versa.
No matter what you plan,
Life has its own plan for you.
Success will fetch you to the world,
Failure will fetch the world to you.
Hope and Faith are the wheels of
Life motor.
Felt that when I have this, the time has gone.
Felt that I was late with the time cycle.

True was that because I was behind things.
Now I go with the flow.
I am not late, not early.
I am very much on time.
I flow with the time, and life is easy now.

15. Be a Tree

Stay grounded.
Connect with your roots.
Turn over a new leaf.
Get Seasoned.
Let the old leaves fall off in Autumn.
Choose your Autumn pivotally.
Grow every Year.
Be the shadow for others.
Bend before you break.
Enjoy the unique beauty.
Have your own shape.
Keep spreading.
Keep growing.

16. A kind of love

It is the kind of love
That could not be
Explained.
It was all these feelings
With no name.
Maybe, I try but can't verbalize.
Maybe that is what love is.
What I see in her,
Wanting, needs, beauty, companionship,
No, No! It is just she,
I look at her and feel something.
That's all.
Do I want her! Need her!
No, I just want her to keep living,
So that my eyes can see her.
I want her to stay happy,
She is damn beautiful when she is happy,
Laughing in and out,
Her eyes shine,
She glows,
My soul is happy with her,
Content that she exists.
She is a Kind, I always wonder whether ever existed!

I believe now. She is a wonder,
A wonder of soul.
A person with an intimate connection,
It clicks, flows, vibes and thrills,
Drawn closer and closer,
The experience of love, so deep, so strong, and complex,
So complex that triggers you to doubt,
Ever did I ever love anybody before!
She connects simply, understands and responds,
Brings ease and purity,
Spreads happiness all around.
The heart is at peace.
Something inexplicable.
Something that brings me back home.
Something that makes me feel more like myself in all the places
I can never have a name for… until now.

17. A Small Step

You may feel like
It is a mountain,
But you sometimes carry a mountain,
That you simply needed to climb.
Doubts, Questions, Fear,
Will come,
Think Big,
Take the first step,
Slowly, gradually, you will make it.
You may feel like not taking the risk
See the sun behind,
Keep going.
Keep on.
Keep marching.
The courage of the small steps,
Will lead you to newer confidence,
Will open new directions,
Will help you have a clearer idea.
Keep on.
You will the bravery, the spirit in you,
The fire in you,
March ahead, don't stop,
Breathe and feel the bliss,

The bliss of chance,
The bliss of a new start,
The bliss of trial,
Don't ever overlook
The power of a small step.
Those small steps are you today
Some day in the past,
You had the same fear,
Look again on you,
You have grown brighter and smarter.
Don't overlook
the power of small steps
Those steps will change your life.
Start small. Keep on. Keep up.

18. Walking in the Wilderness

I find solace amongst the cypress trees;
In the arms, of nature's grasp,
Where catcalls sing cheerful warbles.
Far beyond the deafening drone of business,
The mechanical thrum of mortal noise;
The screaming of the megacity,
And the cries of little girls and boys.
On a rustic bench beside the water,
In a place that only we know,
Magic recollections were vocally planted;
In the auditoriums of our minds, they grow.
Where the seed of love formerly picked
Under the shade of our favorite mulberry tree,
Our love did bloom and grow,
And a beautiful flower came to be.
Walking in nature,
Searching deep within my muddled mind,
Revealed to me, the retired verity,
Which I've endured finding.
It was there inside my secret theater,
In the solace of the cypress trees.
I felt true love's grasp again,

In nature's sweet serenity.

19. Change

Progress may look like
Waking up at six
Instead of eight.
A new beginning may look
As if nothing much has changed.
Love may feel like
What's so unique about this.
Victories may seem
Fruitless and small,
Noone else but you know
Little things seem nothing
But they give peace,
Like those meadow flowers seem orderless separately,
But together they perfume the air.
What is the nature of the change,
How much energy you put into,
How you feel about it,
How long you have been wanting this change,
Nonetheless,
Honor your journey
Celebrate them.

20. All your 2-morrows

Don't make it today just another day.
Take the chance,
Learn something new
Go off track,
Hit the road, Play loud,
Get out of the c-zone,
Find a new comfort zone.
Allow small changes,
Coffee today not tea, right today, not left,
Alone today, no pal,
My today, not us, anything.
If you still try to figure out
What your goals are for life,
Ensure you enjoy the journey in today.
Last year, you said
Next year.
Last month, you said
Next month
Yesterday, you said
Tomorrow.
Today is today, all your
Tomorrows are tomorrows.
Do it now. sometimes 'later' becomes 'never'.

Make 2-morrow, Today. Your day. The Present Day.

21. Manageable!

Don't really know who needs to hear this,
But maybe all of us,
People who try,
People Who never give up,
People who live up for their families,
Without screaming and complaints.
Trust me, things are manageable;
Because you have got to manage them,
Because you have been doing this for years,
So you are very much eligible to manage that,
Because you now know how it is to be managed,
That's why it is manageable, yeah!
Everything is manageable;
Neither life have to fall into pieces, your hopes
Nor you.
Sometimes it is hard to see it-
your mind is clouded with doubts and dares,
But believe me, it is manageable,
Because you have got to do this.
Because you don't have any choice but to manage,
And that's why you make it work.
That is how it is manageable.
The drop of troubles is your reward in the cycle..!

Keep managing!

22. Be that kind

Be that kind of person
Who is not afraid to help
Who is not afraid to ask someone
If they are okay twice if they say they are,
Because you could see they aren't.
Be that kind of person
Who smiles at people with a spread of love.
Be that kind of person
Who prays for people even when they don't.
Be that kind of person
Who is brave enough to express the feelings,
And always proud to love others.
Be that kind of person
Who is strong enough to stand alone in the crowd.
Be that kind of person
Who will correct the action to be a better self.
Be that kind of person
Who is ready to change to make a relationship work.
Be that kind of person
Who breaks the cycle.
If you were judged,
Choose understanding
If you were rejected,

Choose acceptance.
If you were ashamed,
Choose compassion.
Be that person you needed in need,
Not the one who hurt you.
Be that person to vow to be better
Than what broke you.
Be that person who heals,
And not hurts.
Be that kind of person
Who is there for others
Because this is what this world needs.
More of kind-hearted and loving people.

23. Change Something

Change something
Change it yourself.
Let it go.
Change the channel.
Turn it off or on.
Unsubscribe.
Unfollow.
Unfriend, if you wish to.
Mute or block, if you need to.
Do whatever it takes for you to simply
Live and love back yourself.
Remember to do that maturely,
Without
arguments, questions,
doubts, humiliation.
Do that like a matured soul.
Heal inside.
Walk Away.
Breathe.
Travel.
Come home peacefully.

24. Silence Means…

My silence means
I am tired
Tired of arguing,
Explaining
Making it work,
Alone,
Tired of fighting for us.
My silence means
I am tired of
Expressing my feelings to you,
That they exist.
Now they fluctuate too!
My silence means
I don't have the energy
To explain them anymore,
To ask for any more,
To wait for any more.
My silence means
I don't have any complaints now.
My silence means
I am on self-healing and not on blaming anybody,
I am on my real journey of self now.
My silence means

I prefer to let it flow naturally,
I prefer to let it vibe naturally,
without any push or force.
Let it be.
My silence means,
I am done with all.
I had enough of all.
I am done with those cycles.
My silence means,
I prefer to be happier,
With myself,
My dignity,
My power and energy.
Now, I save them for my own good.
My silence means better than my words may try.
Listen and Move on.

25. Bad Chapters

Chapters lengthen life,
The turns - ins and outs, gawky, thorny, and what not
Seasons of shadow, light, and darkness though
Keeps repeating the cycle; bad by the good, good by the bad,
Keep going, hope awaits you.
No matter you wander,
Wonders don't stop
You discern and keep up the journey
The light may head up:
Alone or alone; the alters remains the same
You are alone on this journey.
Wander what bad we have
What good comes by
They say - 'nuggets'
Indeed, a plethora of hundreds of notions, and
What not!
Options; alas, not any, keep going.
Chapters of life; be good or bad
Reveals to us
The secrets of living
A living death, or a dying life.
Bad Chapters, may create great stories,
Like wrong paths may still lead to the right places,

Failed dreams can still create successful people,
As sometimes it takes losing you to find a better you.
Keep going! the chapters won't change the title-
Be sure, that the story will change.
A better story. Be the Maker.
Make the best of it.
This time.
Not to miss, this will not happen again.
Make it yours.

26. I Distraught

Worry? oh, I feel I am the sole proprietor!
I worry a lot: will this happen, will my plant grow, will this work,
Will I fit, will I be able to, will this benefit,
Will pollution reduce, and; will inflation go down:
The song of mourning goes on and on
I knew then- i felt so, it was taught to think and then to act,
Learning now what I need to unlearn:
Some patterns, some perceptions, some you, and some me
Was I right, was I wrong, will I forget, will I forgive,
Can it be worse, or better. Let it go, oh why, let me take it.
Will these streams help, will the advice be true, will the rain be,
Will the yellow leaf turn green again or will fade away.
Can I be a singer, a painter, a teacher,
I see a movie; and feel like being an actress, can I be;
Roads and engineers, poor learning and a teacher,
Parenting and a parent, chaotic and manager,
Home and a home-maker…
I wonder- can I do that all, loops and holes…
Hopeless.
I observed closely, neatly, precisely- repeatedly-
Eyes were overworking,

So now gonna rest for the whole of time: spectacles
Rough, blurry, and foggy world…!
Will my eyesight be clear again, will I lose weight, will I be a writer,
Am I going to get any disease like them?
Fibromyalgia, Alzheimer, disorders,
Will I be using Breast prosthesis !!
endometriosis, alopecia? and so on..
By and by, I've come to know that this process won't stop
Worrying this or that had come to nothing;
Nothing, other than, worrying that I worried,
And I gave it up. happily.
Took the power back, with my old arms in my hand and
Confidence in the head,
Head high, clear sigh, and went out.
What I saw, was
A normal sunny day; 'normal' people, walking around,
And that inside and out: is normal now.
Normal- a rare finding: out and in.
And I say 'better luck' to myself.

27. Broken Wings

Why can't we simply hold on
To one another's hands,
This time will be the last
I fear except I make it very understandable!
I can't win, I can't rule
I shan't dominate this match;
With you,
Take these broken wings.
Figure out how to fly once more;
We hear the voices sing
The cheers today, will reach you tomorrow,
For now,
Take these broken wings.
I can't rest, I can't battle,
I can't eradicate, so I shall assume my faults;
I can't concede we are rasping on one another,
We can't stop now, we can cure the disease of misunderstanding
I can't take one increasingly restless night,
Without you, what is more left,
Let us be in, or
Take these broken wings.
It's all known,

We are half substance, without intimacy,
Without you, what is more, this flesh and blood I am,
So take these wrecked wings with you.
Let's figure out - how shall we fly again,
Separate together, or together separate,
Let's figure out how to live so free,
All are lost, and so are we,
Jobs futile, endeavors futile,
I won't run, I won't fly,
I will never make it by,
Without you,
Take these broken wings.
I won't take off, I won't climb,
In case you're not here, I'm incapacitated,
Without you,
I can't look, I'm so visually impaired,
I lost my heart, I lost my brain,
Without you, without you,
You're all alone.
The crow flies straight,
An ideal line,
On the villain's way,
Until you kick the bucket,
Take these broken wings.
This life is short,
More, that's true,
Better live it right,

You can't return,
Get raise some hellfire,
Before they bring you down,
Take these broken wings
Get carry on with this life
Till you kick the bucket
You better have the soul
Out and about ahead
Take these broken wings.

28. Call Me Anytime

Wandering like you, me, and us;
What the strange world we live in,
I stand alone to observe you,
Amidst the crowd and the street,
Is that you?!
Know, I know, what it is,
How it is,
I feel what you feel,
The loved ones you have lost,
The years which have been a loss of youth
The tears that your pillow has caught
Know, I know that all.
Do I spell them, do I need to
Oh, maybe, yes and no, someday.
My travel on your journey remains the same,
Alas! not yours.
Though call me any time;
Without fear of judgment or pity,
I shall hold you like a friend,
As I am.
I shall fake not the words,
My warmth may speak for me,
My actions will have your faith:

Trust, and retain that,
Call me, call me to you,
I shall be by your side,
Rain and night,
Dry and hard,
Rough and spur
Will be and will I, be by your side.
Call me anytime, call me in your pain,
That knows me, have been with it since long,
We are a good companion!
I shall take that with me,
Will leave you relieved of the scratches and all burdon.
Call me, not for I can be a reason to smile,
But for I can cry with you,
Call me, not because I shall guide you on how to overcome,
But for I understand how badly that pains.
Call me, I shall be you:
To cry, laugh, spell, went and wipeout
Call me anytime, I will be you for you,
And yours forever,
For the pain, you endeavor,
I know them all: I have been to them,
I know how that feels,
So I shall try, at least.
Call me anytime, because I know how it feels to have or not have
Call me because I know not to hurt when you get hurt,

Call me b'cause, it is not a deal, it is just me,
Without hopes and highs:
Because I am your friend.

29. I Adore You

You! Lord of my life, governor of generations
I designate you on the peak of respect,
Oh, my teacher,
Your words make my heart feel full of joy,
Recalled to memory,
Finer and encouraging,
Triggers me to be me,
I adore you.
How blessed I was,
You descended upon life's lake, like a light moon,
Under winter's sun, like a warm confort.
In you, stays all my faith and pride,
My peace, my honor.
I shall be your dream to come true
Forever, close like dream to eyes.
I adore you for what I m today.
Those nights and days,
Minutes and moments,
Spent behind,
To bring a child to a grown woman,
I adore you.
And you forever be my guide.

30. Won't beg for your Love

I shan't beg for
Your time,
Your energy,
Your essence,
Your efforts,
Your attention,
Your head and hand,
Your eyes and sight,
You and us,
And your love.
I simply withdraw now.
Let me let you go,
And get "my 'me'" come back from you.
I shall not beg now.
I won't.

31. From Sorrow to Joy

The world is too self-centered,
Really it is . . . !
How the air can spoil,
The holy atmosphere.
They approach when they need you,
And become indifferent indeed.
How selfish the world is!
They bring you down
Pinch you, play pranks on you,
They shower the pains,
To retain and make the comforts of their own,
What satisfies them!
The 'Ego', the 'me', and the 'I'.
Be private or work,
We have this around us.
For their or the other sake,
In this or the other form.
What this results into!
Let's break the chain.
Let's stop for a while,
breath for a moment and see, who is behind us.
Stop, then, your chase.
Turn, face, hold.

Hold the hand, the one behind you;
Stood by you, day and night,
Hard and dry,
For you, for "us"
Feel what they feel for you.
See the unconditional in the conditionals around you;
See the love in them,
Show the love in you.
Make a circle, be the center of beauty.
Be "us".
There you go, to find
A small and beautiful world,
A world that we create, we can and we could create,
Off the boundaries of strata, age, culture, and words,
Be the world of beauty in and out.
The world of joy, then
Awaits you,
Welcomes you.
See the sunshine, break the chain,
Stop and turn.
See your world.
Simplify and Satisfy the soul.
Stop chasing.
Relax and breathe.
See the journey of self-growth
See the path you have traveled
From sorrow to joy.

32. It is Clear!

Let me be clear;
Your disconnection is okay,
But not the ignorance.
Your being busy is okay,
But not the callous attitude.
Your disagreements are okay,
But not the disrespect.
Your distance is okay,
But not the disloyalty.
My love is unconditional,
But not your presence in life.
Your re-prioritizing is okay,
But putting me down is not.
Falling in love with
The souls;
With scars and pain,
The beauty of real, in and out,
The rawness in them,
The wealth of emotions,
Their tears and laughter
Falling in love with
The nuggets and compassion.
The kindness and oneness. It is clear.

33. Be Sensitive.

Break out with,
'Being sensitive is impractical.'
Being sensitive is being practical.
Being practical is a need to do
What you need to do at the moment,
With a situation.
Don't offer a lecture to someone
Who needs a hug.
Don't be angry on someone,
Who needs your touch.
Don't let them lose hope in you,
Because you're trying to settled down.
Try to settle the mind and a heart in you,
To better settle down with your relations,
With your people.
Don't be hesitant to say them
You love them.
Don't be afraid to say
What you feel, what you think.
What they mean to you.
Caring is not a being crazy.
Don't be ashamed of your feelings,
For they make you unique,

For they are part of you,
They are you.
Let them know you like them.
Let them know they inspire you.
Let them know, they look good in this or that attire.
Let them know, they look good when they smile.
Tell your mother you love her and her motherhood,
Her food and her care.
Tell your father, you wait for him every day to watch TV together.
Tell your sister you miss her.
Tell your brother, you are still willing to exchange the pair of clothes,
Tell your friend you value them like your family.
Tell that made you appreciate her organized way,
Tell that neighbor, you have noted the regular by-door concern.
Tell that colleague when you miss him/her on the day of their day-off.
Let the words come out of your mouth
Let the world be the world of words,
Let the world outside see the beauty of spells,
Spell and roll, feel and bless,
See the magic of being at ease of words.
It is beautiful to feel and express,
It is beautiful to live the emotions,
It is beautiful to feel the rain drop on the cheeks and palm,

It is beautiful to close the eyes,
See a face, Smile, breathe and feel.
It is breathtakingly beautiful in the moments of smaller magic,
Occurs when you strop down,
And are honest with yourself and others.
there is sensible beauty in.
it is beautiful to be sensitive. Stay beautiful.

34. If We Meet Age'n

If we meet again as strangers
I shall re-know not, I shall know you better.
If we meet ag'n,
I shall learn to appreciate you more.
If we meet ag'n,
I shall listen to you more,
More attentively, more peaceful.
If we meet ag'n,
I shall admit my follies.
If we meet ag'n,
I shall bring flowers and chocolates,
the normal day,
To make your mundane a happy day.
If we meet ag'n,
I shall be more courteous and respectful.
If we meet ag'n,
I shall be less me and more you.
For not that I want to impress you,
but for I have known your worth.
For not that I don't have option,
But for I know what I have found in you.
If we meet ag'n,
I shall make it work. For us.

FORAM PATEL

35. Live before you Leave

'Son, we want to go to pilgrimage'
Without tickets, they have left.
On the journey of the universe.
'Hey, let's plan a trip!'
And that friend has met with an accident,
He has left aboard forever.
'No, not this year, lets plan after I settle'
My brother said, and he has settled for heavily bliss,
May be on some other planets,
Leaving us here on the earth.
We are trying to settle ourselves down.
Mine and many other stories,
People have gone.
Many are in queue,
We are dying in a hole.
Every minute someone is struggling between life and death,
Every second someone is leaving this world behind.
We are in the line without knowing it.
We never know how many people are
After and before us.
Can we move the lines!
We cannot move to the back of the line.
We cannot avoid the line.

So. . .
Change the punctuations,
So while we wait in the line -
Make moments count.
Make priorities.
Make time to do things you like.
Make your gifts known.
Count your blessings.
Make your people feel special.
Make your voice heard.
Roar and start the journey.
Make the small things big.
Make someone smile.
Take off and relax.
Make a change for the day.
Make up.
Make peace;
With yourself and others.
Make sure you have put it right.
Make sure to tell them they are loved.
Make sure to have no regrets.
Make sure you are ready.
Before you realize it is too late.
Live it before you leave.

Writer's Message

Dear All,

When it comes to life, we try to define and get the things settled everytime we face them. Having said that we keep waiting for good days to come which may come or may not. The beauty of life lies in its unpredictability. Imagine, you know everythings about your life, you will end up mundane, tiring, boring, tedious. Life is what we have. It is the feeling you have of being alive on this earth. You can smell, touch, see, feel, walk and so forth. And in the journey of this livingness, we create ourselves, we know ourselves, we improve ourselves, and we live ourselves this or the other ways.

So, let's live up to the most possible way and stay ready for whatever is to come.

Don't give up on life. It is one time or never.

Love.

You may write your feedback to foram.digitalaura@gmail.com

Printed by Libri Plureos GmbH in Hamburg,
Germany